SEEING YOU AGAIN

SEEING YOU AGAIN

BY STEVE CLORFEINE

OPEN HOUSE PRESS
New York

ALSO BY STEVE CLORFEINE

Beginning Again
In the Valley of the Gods
Field Road Sky
While We Were Dancing
Together/Apart
Simple Geometry

OPEN HOUSE PRESS
New York

First Edition

Printed in the United States of America
© 2023 Steve Clorfeine

ISBN 979-8-9875585-0-8

All rights reserved. No part of this publication protected by this copyright notice may be reproduced or utilized in any form or by any means, electronic, mechanical, including photocopying, recording or by any information storage and retrieval system, without written permission of the publisher.

To Lanny
who first brought me to East Meredith

To Sarah
ever the muse

TABLE OF CONTENTS

Still	3
Winter Haiku	4
Grouse	7
Dharma	8
First Rain	9
May 2020, early Pandemic	10
But Maybe	12
Jasper	13
June Morning	14
June Morning 2	15
July Fourth 2020	16
Here, Over There	17
Midsummer Haiku	18
Scattered	19
Atlantic Beaches	23
What If	24
Contemplate	25
Patience	27
Anita Dying	28
Words I /L. E. translates from Homer	30
Words II / This or That	31
Words III	32
Words IV	33
Words V / Mother	34
Words VI / About July	35
All The Dogs	36
Sitting	37
Then and Now	38
Friend Rumi	40
February Hawk	41
Coming Out	42
Becoming	44
Reverie/Study	45
We Meet Again	46

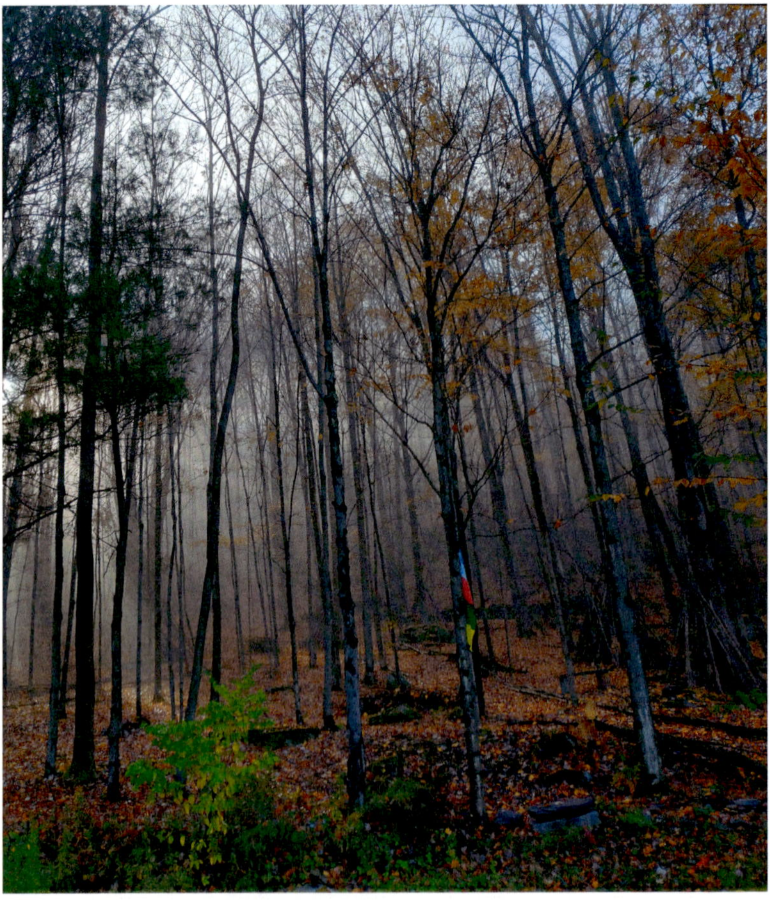

I. East Meredith, 2020-2022

Doing nothing at the center of everything
John Tarrant, Roshi

Still

a solitary time
not only winter
but the world split apart

branches in the woods cross
willy nilly
like waking from a dream

again everything as it was
same time same place
fat robin on a slender branch

Winter Haiku

in fading light I read Soen's poems
close the book when I can
no longer see the words

asleep, then momentarily awakened
only to drift back
what I call my life

everything settles
deep snow still
postbox half buried

bare branches
gray sky
tonight's snow womb

bottom on one chair
legs up on another
tinkling water in heat pipes

sitting
waiting for night
endless dusk

delicate snow on tough spruce
my will bends to the weather

what aches more
this aging body or
its shifting heart

snow again, then sleet
time of no decision
only ice

old friend habit disturbed this morning
I go through without bread or butter
forgetting day forgetting dates
until another one arises
dark night in early morning

simple things: a shawl wrapped around legs
my comfortable chair
gaze onto snow fogged horizon
into windswept sashay of trees

is there a purpose
heart beats
breathe
I follow

snowfall fairytale windless
I place the dead bird in a crevice
beneath a boulder

full moon
year's end
dark snow shadows
stars scatter rainbow dust
through the woods

Soen Nakagawa, Zen priest, Haiku master 1908-1984

Grouse

only trees, only snow
only the dead bird frozen on the porch
where I protect her, measure her
turn her every which way to know her better

she came crashing through a pane in the garage door
I was away there'd been a storm
big snow winds she lost her bearings

no blood just her
stiff & silent on a mat in the corner
shards of glass everywhere

I place her half buried in the snow
the next day bring her up to the porch
so I can visit her

before leaving for the month
I carry her to a crevice under a boulder
where she lies until the April thaw
when the fox takes her

Dharma

ordinary things:
slate sky
tattered cushion
worn leather boots

a long ago fallen tree
blackened by time & holding
pools of bright moss

how they are meant for each other
moss & tree
dying & growing

Kobin Chino says
like two minds riding out together

Kobin Chino, Zen master, calligraphy master 1938-2002

First Rain

Drifting clouds
sting of wind
no alarm, just sting
fingers, shoulders, toes in boots

Imagine warmth
stay with clouds, with first
light drops on scalp

May 2020, early Pandemic

lucky with the new birdfeeder
the first week or two
until red squirrels find their way up
hang by their toes, a circus act, no big deal
frantic, they chuck the seed & somehow
don't offend the small birds
whose territory it had been

by week three the seed goes quickly &
the squirrels, in search of more
break open the red container & feast

the following week a bear
tips the bird feeder off its hangar
& takes off with it

we are living a new way
thinking it temporary like the snow squalls
this eighth day of May
the bare woods bare of leaves pushing out
lilac buds sturdy if not frozen

hold tight the spread, the dying, the disbelievers
our own solitude in a house on a dirt road
easy to dissemble

I tell a friend I spend a quarter of my time
wandering around the house & he replies
is that all?

we retreat from spring back to winter
dust off snow push back the porch furniture
take in wood from under tarpaulins where
even today, wishing spring along
I'd made a contest out of not using any of that pile

But Maybe

but maybe now this is spring

blue jays at the feeder
bully their smaller mates
knock seed onto the ground and
later will attack the apple trees

but when my wife spots a pair of them
gently pecking their beaks together
(silhouettes on a branch against an
impatient bare landscape)
she speaks of it with such delight
praising high their jay blue flash

the next day I change my mind

Jasper

Up the road a billy-goat, penned in beside a red farmhouse. At my approach it lets out a shrill cry, to which I call back, best I can. I think it works because he lifts his forelegs onto the fence and shrieks even louder. What am I thinking? He can easily jump the fence and here he is, poised to make the leap. I'd like to see that but then he'd be out on the road. So I quietly talk to him, talk him down. Or so I imagine. He appears to relax.

On the walk back down the road, a gray pick-up turns into the red farmhouse driveway. I recount my conversation with the billy-goat.

Yup, he says, *that's Jasper. I often wonder why he doesn't jump the fence.*

June Morning

At the foot of the driveway
I tend day lilies
watch them rise to morning sun

In patterns of sleep & wake
I rise to morning aches
the in between
residue of dreams in which persons so vivid
they accompany me from room to room

Faithfully I meditate
tea by my side
chair on the back porch
facing the shrine of the woods
or the indoor shrine
water bowls, incense
photos of dharma teachers

All alive at the three times gong

June Morning 2

Dead mouse left in daylight
likely to be eaten by fox
in the firefly night

At dawn next day crow eats mouse
how did fox miss it last night?

Step out into mist six a.m.
groundhog scrambles under garage
wild turkey band marches the woods
little ones camouflaged beneath tall ferns

Meanwhile I examine a hornet nest
is it empty?
listen for buzzing but not too close

Pileated woodpecker
early to work this morning
pause in its hammering
then small peeps from a nearby nest

The neighbor's dog barks
I look down surprised at a dark streak of dirt
across my white tee-shirt &
remember picking lettuce
shaking pools of rainwater from its folds

July Fourth 2020

July Fourth
a day to look for truce
(or do I mean truth)
instead, demons of disappointment

woke up & said to myself
what are we independent from?

time slims down
one day next day
thoughts, a revolving door
I go in and out

still, the raised beds of greens are full
the land is flush with summer
exhale and bow
as full moon rises

Here, Over There

It's mid-summer &
next to an open window
she plays Shubert on the piano

our carpenter friend Tjalling
stops banging
comes down the hill &
lies under the window to listen

out west, Texas near the Mexican border
windows in the children's detention center
locked shut & there is always a child wailing

how do we fit this country
land of the free
land of the free for all
crowded tears & blasphemy

house wren, nuthatch, titmouse
small migrants on their way about

we are constant gardeners
amidst our own wreckage

Midsummer Haiku

only yesterday
dark clouds' promises
again forgotten

two wing beats
robin's flight from nest
to Buddha's head

Peake's Bridge Rd. splits
& neither fork gets me
where I want to go

who left who behind
was a big question
years later, only relief

Scattered

I'm jumpy at the howl of a dog

Some days I leave the house only to
pick up mail down the driveway
sweep stacks of maples leaves off stone steps

Open the screen door and all at once
a flock of sparrows beat their wings &
tiny mottled brown bodies swell into flight

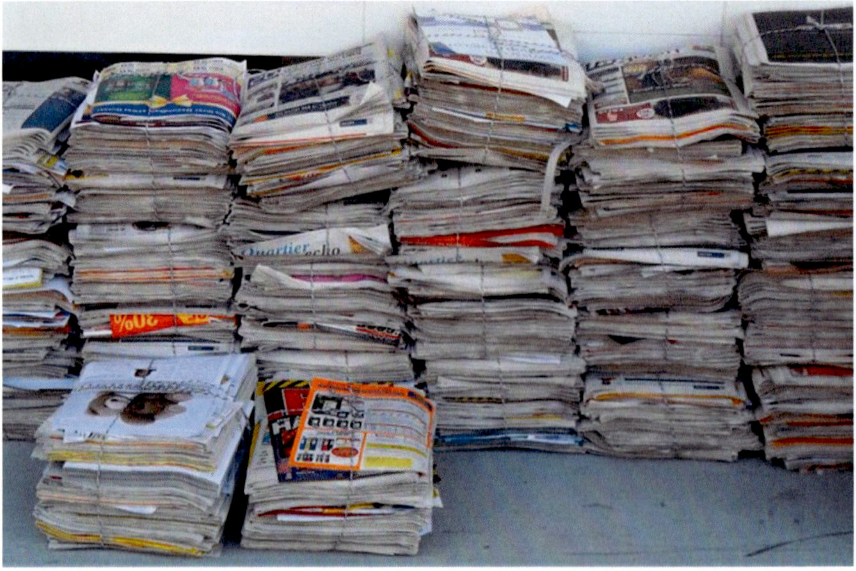

II. Anyday Journal - Notes and Poems

To live in the swarm of human speech
Robert Duncan

Atlantic Beaches

Atlantic dunes follow
prompts of wind and sea
drift their delicate bulk of sand

the sea too, its fathom of motives
waves mount, crest, collapse

like dolphins tossed on waves
of their own making
my spirit soars and quiets
soaked in Trungpa's crazy wisdom

inland I think of Odysseus
ever homesick
not wanting to forget

and Rumi's line I love
late by myself in the boat of myself

these days I'm saturated with damp moods
would like to mop myself up

Christopher Isherwood writes
(and this too is on my mind)
homesickness for sanity is the only reason
to take up a spiritual discipline

What If

What if our imperfections
were islands in their own symmetry
washed away
only to return
to be washed away
once more

Of the ones he loved
he longs for the secret of them
inside his skin
& what's beneath the surface

Contemplate

Joaquin, the hurricane with a beautiful name
I walk miles in its wind and rain &
next day I'm speedy, off balance
dreams wash up on a moment's notice

Chogyam writes
clean up your own shit
....

Individually examining
third aspect of patience in
Buddhist methodology

You are the method, I tell myself
preparing for a meditation class
....

Again I consider
revulsion is the foot of meditation
putting one's foot on the path each time

& make a note that expectations
are loose footing & all the same
you can't do anything wrong
....

In the workshop I tell the students:
off-center is good, maybe better
you know where to go from there

Chogyam Trungpa, Tibetan meditation master
and master artist 1940-1987

Patience

At the stadium track in the small city a young father twirls a kid size football in one hand and watches his three year old leap and fall into the long jump sand pit.

Each time I circle the track I glance over. The father would like the boy to take some interest in the football but the boy continues to slide and lay face down in the sand.

On my next lap around I notice the father doing squats, the child still on his belly in the sand. I think about my Buddhist refuge name, *goldsun of patience* and about teachings on waiting, waiting until things ripen.

Anita Dying

The car door closes quietly enough. Everything hushed. I don't feel the breeze until I'm startled by the crunch of leaves underfoot.

She is dying and being who she is, living strong in dying.

I notice the faded yellow paint this side of her house, the unstained two by four on the railing, webs of cracks in the cement.

Alive, everything is alive. My awkwardness climbing the steps, readying to meet a dying friend.

Until now she was in treatment, in remission, years like that, always going forward, always being present.

Her living room is filled with flowers. She chuckles about the hothouse bouquets which dominate the room and smiling, points to a vase of the last November wildflowers, whatever was blooming down the road.

Her voice gains strength as we talk about what we always talk about. How she made that vase, the one with the November wildflowers, how I'm making vases again. A painting of hers I've never seen before. *Oh yes* she says, *I took that down from the attic. I'd forgotten about it.*

She is quick and lively and talking only about living, about walking every day, about the doctor wanting to see her next week, that she doesn't know why.

There's something in that *why* that says more than she will speak about. Her fine boned face is more gaunt than the last time; her long fingers papery, her mid-section covered in blankets.

Let me make sure I have your number in this new phone I have. Moments after I drive down the road, there's a text from her. *Hi there. Loved the visit. Maybe bring one of the new vases to show me if we visit again.*

Words I /L. E. translates from Homer

The waters fell asleep at midnight

Not receding or raising their voice
but evidently & simply without warning
the waters close their waves
quiet the remaining ripples and drift off

Praise the sea
the skiff, its mates inside
their watery cosmology

Gills & fine bones
puckered lips
evanescent skins

A sea of imaginary words
washed ashore
in alphabetical order
conjunctions swallowed by seahorses
who expel glorious sounds
not mere gurgles but seductive melodies

Words II / This or That

a familiar conversation:
he wants, she wants
who does the most does it best
who is polite, who's gloomy
is it really possible?

boils down to:
sleeping in a cave
might be a good idea

Words III

Hours after the children are asleep
I wake searching for what happens
when the preacher on the hill takes the piggy's ring &
marries pussycat to owl. I will. I do.

A friend is able to speak again years after writing notes.
I don't ask but wonder does he recognize his voice as the
vocal resurrection begins.

A friend sends a book called *The Lost Words*
words eliminated from the Junior Oxford Dictionary:
otter heron acorn willow heather raven
so many poems lost right then & there

I get serious about making better use of words:
*offer them up as nurses to the infirmary for wounded
language.*

Words IV

what came first
destiny, fate or a
complex idea like karma

for her it was music
for him, water

words by nature elusive
melancholy a feeling where words leave off
even the sadness is not yours my friend

for example what came before
written on the behavior column
of his fourth grade report card:
shows improvement

Words V/Mother

My mother's slanted script on a yellow slip of
Board of Education paper she's brought home
from her classroom supply cupboard

penciled note left on kitchen table
instructions for me to follow
to get dinner ready after school

at 4:30 set oven to 350 for ten minutes
take dish covered in foil out of frig
place on top rack set timer for 30 minutes
when timer rings turn oven off and leave
dish on rack I'll be back by 5:30

………………..

An interviewer asks where I was born
I begin to answer when my mother interrupts
No, she says in a sharp tone
I was driving & when I went into labor
I didn't go to the hospital. I went to the beach.
You were born on the beach.

(which explains everything)

Words VI/About July

Lush this July
verdant wet breezy

Simple poems sedate by day
but at night words fly wild
like cumulus cloud
behave like specters in early morning
when they refuse captivity

During meditation
I look down at my bare feet
which seem not to belong to me this morning

All The Dogs

Dreams were episodic and I wondered why I kept on
with it. Hours more until the phone rang.
Had I forgotten yesterday's meeting? Well yes, I had.
Apologized and despite the dreams I wanted more sleep.

The heat was up and it wasn't so bad to get out of bed.

I sat warming my hands on the teacup watching nimble
leaves wave across the window.

Heard a car revving, then the neighbor's dog then
another dog.
Thought about all the dogs in my life.
And the dead puppy Jock in *Forbidden Games*.

Sitting

I roll to the middle of the bed where you
are absent & the cool sheet unwrinkled

I lie in the hammock
drift off to tropics where no one
speaks my language
(alone inside a mosquito net
I rock myself to sleep)

I sit under wet maples
which splash lightly all around &
breeze unbidden moistens my bare arms

these days I have no answer
the words of the poet
weeping and laughing at once

Then and Now

first baguettes of the day
Rue le Goff onto Rue Soufflot
early morning walk to class
Rue L'Homond off the Pantheon
the markets and nightclubs of Rue Mouffetard
up steps to the restaurant at the triangle corner
where we bypass the school cafeteria lunch
nineteen & sprung loose

………………..

on the edge of a low cliff above the Adriatic Sea
the camp tent uninviting
the whiskey I was afraid of
heartbroken & no way out of the long night ahead
weeks, months later the darkness that still lay across my young mind

the story of betrayal spilled out to the landlady in Zagreb
she spoke no English & cackled at my Serbo-Croatian
the language I'd never used to such purpose

she went about her business
stood on a stool stirring a cauldron on the stove
down on her stout haunches
prodding the bedsheets into a second cauldron

steam rose and swept the two small rooms

....

my father's navy issue jacket
smoked by ammunition ship fires, 1944
at thirteen, I wear it everyday to school
never sharing its burning secret until
one day my mother gives it to Goodwill

....

Dear Body. First of all, thank you. I know it gets tougher on you, the natural course of thinning out, thickening up, tightening, chipping, stumbling. Most of all forgetting. Nonetheless. Capacity. Even better understanding how the diminished parts work.

Friend Rumi

Behind the waves
of this and that
the space of quiet
accepts the busy other

the moon's place in evening geography:
moving through night to faintly daybreak
coming and going unquestioned
a simple prayer for the wakening light

in small circles we piece our puzzlement
only to misplace and puzzle again

the work begins tomorrow Rumi says
in a poem set in a desert garden
where wife and husband quarrel
through the moonless night

cloud in pale sky
moon in its corner of residence
as ruler of cloud

first we forgive ourselves
that bare familiar place
where dying also lives

February Hawk

I unpack the car, close the garage door and head back down the driveway to check the mailbox. A quarter of the way down, maybe twenty yards away, I'm stopped by a hawk, busy with its meal on the driveway gravel. I imagine it's one of the neighborhood hawks I spot from our kitchen window.

The hawk pecks and pulls at a dead creature. It is voracious. Until this week the snow has been deep.

The hawk doesn't let up, nor is it disturbed by my movement as I inch closer each time street traffic gives me cover. When feathers fly I know the prey is a bird, one of the multitude of sparrows that hang around the tall japonicas that flank the corner of our neighbor's house.

I'm within three yards of the hawk. After each peck or pull, it glances the corner of its hawk eye over at me. Strings of red intestines fly down the hawk's gullet. It clamps its left foot taut on the prey; torque for better ripping and tearing its feast.

The hawk is gone. I feel the body of the dead bird offered up. Shaken by what I feel, I distract myself by remembering the patterns of the hawk's feathers, its underbelly and tail, trusting this will help me name it in the Peterson's Guide.

Coming Out

pocket tornadoes in the spinney wood
slice of maple, slice of spruce, slice of oak
massive bouquets of leaves everywhere
paths unpassable

when the weather clears
a friend brings watermelon
we talk about hummingbirds on geraniums
rabbits under the garage
a single porcupine quill on the front porch
snakes on the woodpile in morning sun

at night fierce winds shake the house
by day, lies show the truth
dreams submerge the horror
until the next night

the same friend
describes his 16 year old son as desultory
& we're both unsure which syllable has the accent

all the same
we long for illumination
certain it's still there
in basements of Kharkiv and Kherson
in hearts of women pregnant from rape
fathers, uncles, brothers gone mad with cruelty

this is who we are my friend says
we're just now coming out of the closet

Becoming

I could live with little
but little by little all these years
so much has come to live around me
& I like it all

The pew in the corner of the room
the ones it was built for
the ones who sat upright on it
knelt onto red cushions &
recited words they'd been taught

Before that
the wood, the tree
the sawyer, carpenter
hands that shaped the pew
the god in our hands

Gradually I give up things
tennis racket, cross country skis, baseball glove
that I won't dance again the way I remember myself

so I give up this
and that
and even myself

I become solicitous
felicitous

Reverie/Study

I lie awake, listen to birds, their squabbling.
Morning approaches.
Approach, like transition, an activity I contemplate.
The movement to another season.
How close a wild animal will get to me or I to it.
Do we see into each other's eyes.

Study
The way things shift
Even passing through doors
I remember I'm here
Not there.

We Meet Again

we meet again
over coffee
over scotch
over time
and time again

make beauty of nothing
as if nothing
ever happened

ACKNOWLEDGEMENTS

Cover photo: Pinsk, Belarus, Sept. 2016
from the balcony of my hotel
Part 1 photo: Woods at our house, 2021
East Meredith, NY
Part 2 photo: Zurich, 2020
Back Cover: Author photo, Christine Alicino

Designed by Cynthia Levine

Thanks to Erika Berland for reading Part 1
and to Wendell Beavers and David Schneider